MY FIRST
HIRAGANA
ACTIVITY BOOK

YUKO GREEN

DOVER PUBLICATIONS, INC.
MINEOLA, NEW YORK

PUBLISHER'S NOTE

With this book you can learn the *hiragana* (Japanese syllables) and more than 330 Japanese words. One or two of the 46 basic *hiragana* symbols appears on each of the pages 2–41, along with several words beginning with that *hiragana*, and pictures of the objects and actions the words represent. Look at the *hiragana* symbols, pronounce the words, and have fun coloring the pictures. A diagram shows you how to write each symbol, and spaces are provided for you to practice writing it.

For people who want to look up an English word quickly in the *hiragana* pages, an index to all English words included in this book has been provided on page 46, following the Japanese/English Word List. For those who want to find a specific *hiragana* syllable rapidly, and the illustrations of words that begin with or contain that syllable, the page number of the corresponding illustration page is given at the beginning of each symbol's word group in the Japanese/English Word List. Also, the 46 basic *hiragana* presented on pages 2–41 appear in the same order as they do in the Hiragana chart on page 1 (reading across each row of the chart, from the top).

Copyright

Copyright © 2000 by Dover Publications, Inc.
All rights reserved.

Bibliographical Note

My First Hiragana Activity Book is a new work, first published by
Dover Publications, Inc., in 2000.

International Standard Book Number

ISBN-13: 978-0-486-41336-5
ISBN-10: 0-486-41336-5

Manufactured in the United States by LSC Communications
41336509   2017
www.doverpublications.com

Hiragana

The *Hiragana* is like a Japanese "alphabet," but each *hiragana* shows a syllable rather than a single letter.

Syllables can be any vowel, **a, i, u, e, o**, or a combination of a vowel plus consonant(s). There are 46 basic *hiragana* symbols.

	a	i	u	e	o
	あ a	い i	う u	え e	お o
k	か ka	き ki	く ku	け ke	こ ko
s	さ sa	し (shi)	す su	せ se	そ so
t	た ta	ち (chi)	つ (tsu)	て te	と to
n	な na	に ni	ぬ nu	ね ne	の no
h	は ha	ひ hi	ふ (fu)	へ he	ほ ho
m	ま ma	み mi	む mu	め me	も mo
y	や ya		ゆ yu		よ yo
r	ら ra	り ri	る ru	れ re	ろ ro
w	わ wa				を (o)
n	ん (n)				

Modified Syllables

が ga	ぎ gi	ぐ gu	げ ge	ご go
ざ za	じ ji	ず zu	ぜ ze	ぞ zo
だ da	(ぢ) ji	(づ) zu	で de	ど do
ば ba	び bi	ぶ bu	べ be	ぼ bo
ぱ pa	ぴ pi	ぷ pu	ぺ pe	ぽ po

きゃ kya	きゅ kyu	きょ kyo
ぎゃ gya	ぎゅ gyu	ぎょ gyo
しゃ sha	しゅ shu	しょ sho
じゃ ja	じゅ ju	じょ jo
ちゃ cha	ちゅ chu	ちょ cho
にゃ nya	にゅ nyu	にょ nyo
ひゃ hya	ひゅ hyu	ひょ hyo
びゃ bya	びゅ byu	びょ byo
ぴゃ pya	ぴゅ pyu	ぴょ pyo
みゃ mya	みゅ myu	みょ myo
りゃ rya	りゅ ryu	りょ ryo

Notes

1. Double vowels are written with (¯,) and should be pronounced a little longer. Examples: ū (うう), ō (おうor おお).
2. No easy Japanese words begin with る. The words in the る section include る in the middle or at the end.
3. を (o) is used only as a particle between other words.
4. ん (n) never begins a word. It is used only in the middle or at the end of a word.
5. Because Hiragana is phonetic, sometimes two words in this book have exactly the same Hiragana spelling, but they are two different words with different meanings. Examples: *kumo* (cloud and spider), *me* (eye and bud).

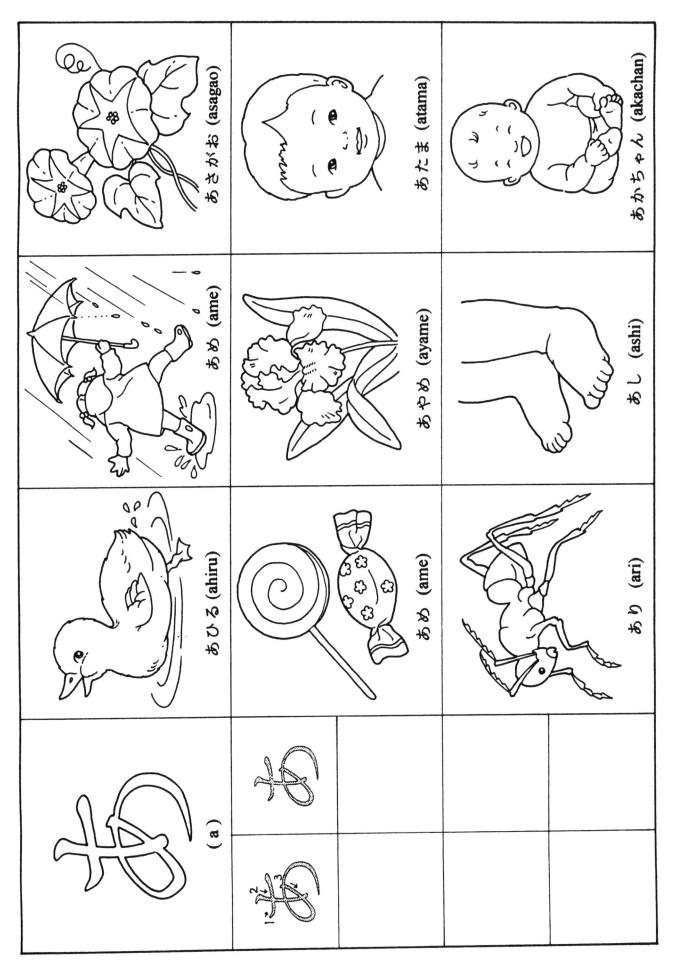

あさがお (asagao)

あたま (atama)

あかちゃん (akachan)

あめ (ame)

あやめ (ayame)

あし (ashi)

あひる (ahiru)

あめ (ame)

あり (ari)

(a)

2

いるか (iruka)

いか (ika)

いのしし (inoshishi)

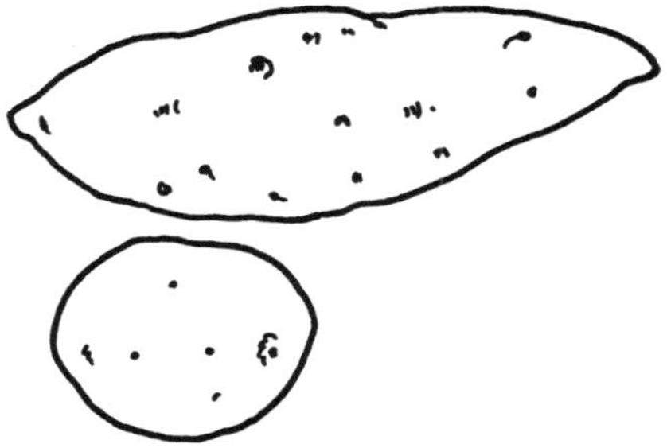

いも (imo)

いえ (ie)

いし (ishi)

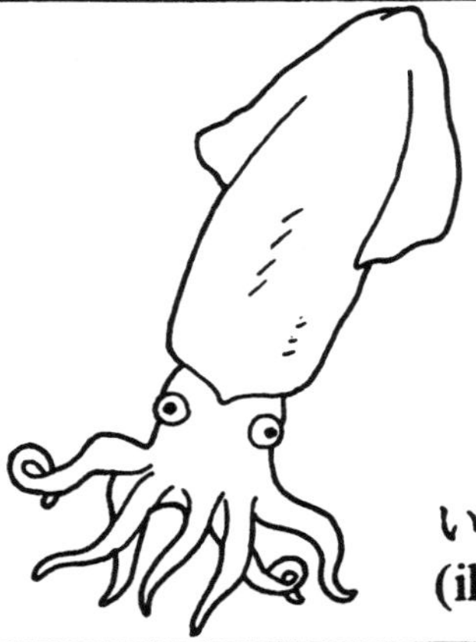

いぬ (inu)

いちご (ichigo)

いす (isu)

い (i)

うま (uma)	うで (ude)	うでどけい (udedokei)
うなぎ (unagi)	うさぎ (usagi)	うちわ (uchiwa)
うし (ushi)	うきわ (ukiwa)	うみ (umi)
（u）		

4

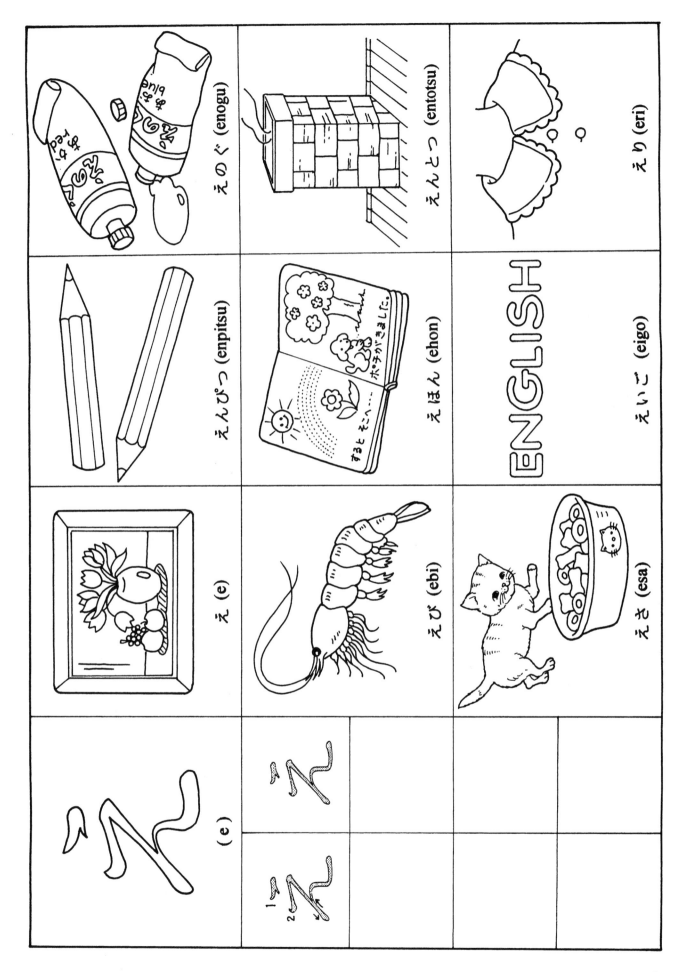

えのぐ (enogu)

えんとつ (entotsu)

えり (eri)

えんぴつ (enpitsu)

えほん (ehon)

えいご (eigo)

え (e)

えび (ebi)

えさ (esa)

(e)

おんなのこ (onnanoko)

おとこのこ (otokonoko)

おおかみ (ōkami)

おもちゃ (omocha)

おかね (okane)

おに (oni)

おりがみ (origami)

おにぎり (onigiri)

おちゃ (ocha)

(o)

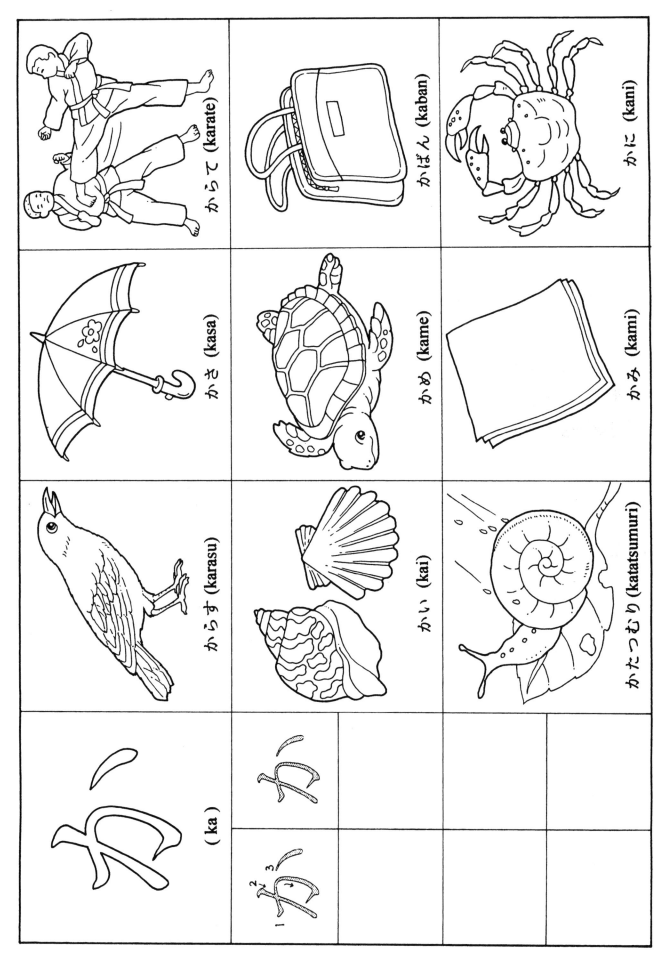

からて (karate)

かばん (kaban)

かに (kani)

かさ (kasa)

かめ (kame)

かみ (kami)

からす (karasu)

かい (kai)

かたつむり (katatsumuri)

か (ka)

き (ki)

きって (kitte)

きのこ (kinoko)

きりん (kirin)

きしゃ (kisha)

きっぷ (kippu)

きつね (kitsune)

きもの (kimono)

きば (kiba)

キ (ki)

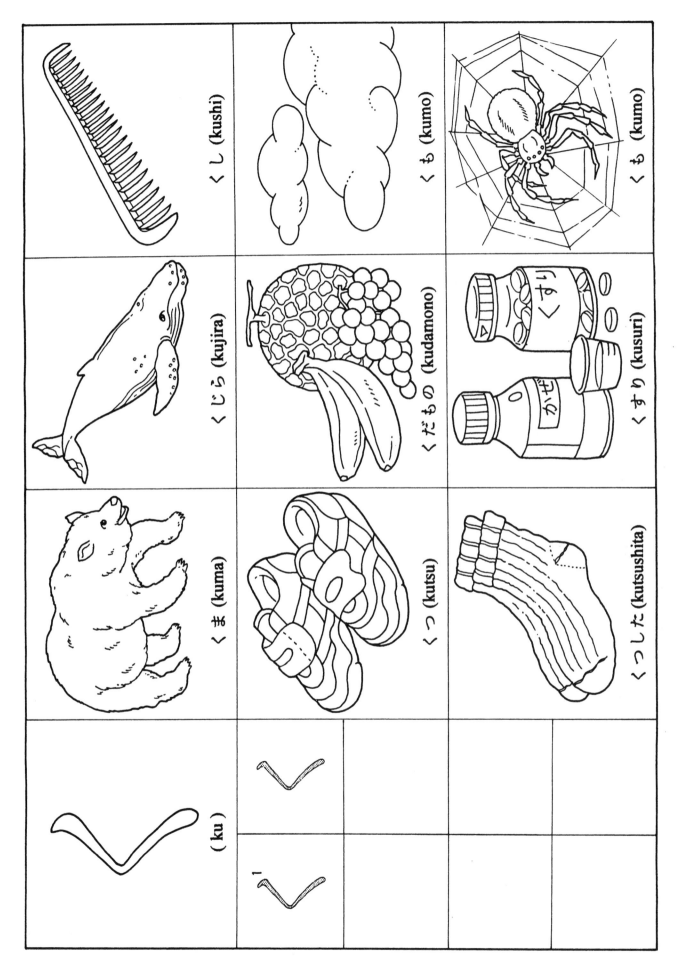

くし (kushi)

くも (kumo)

くも (kumo)

くじら (kujira)

くだもの (kudamono)

くすり (kusuri)

くま (kuma)

くつ (kutsu)

くつした (kutsushita)

(ku)

9

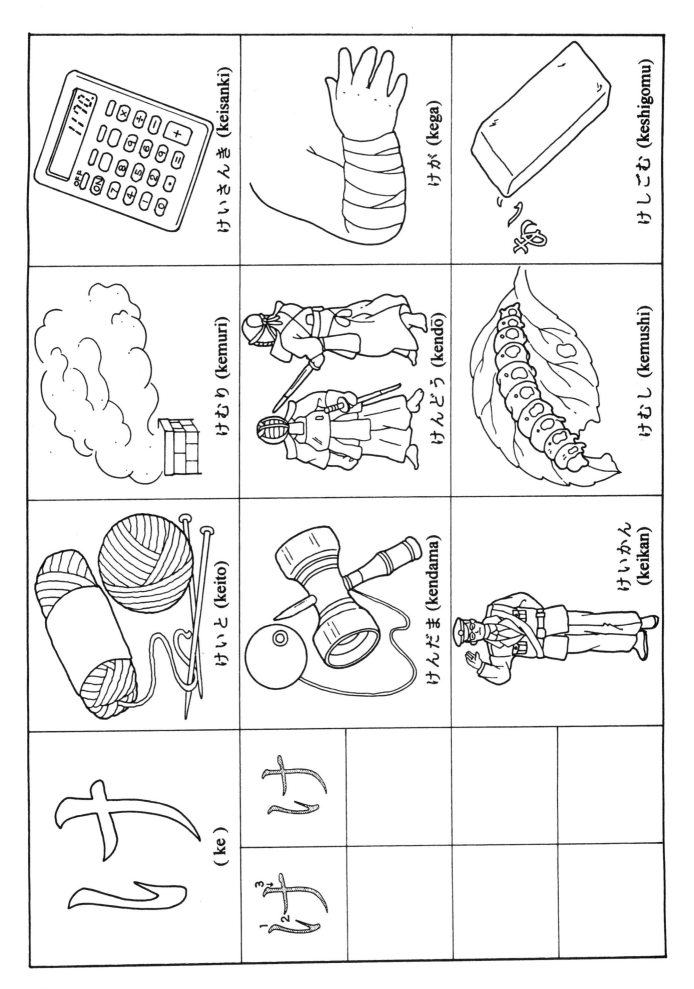

けいさんき (keisanki)

けが (kega)

けしごむ (keshigomu)

けむり (kemuri)

けんどう (kendō)

けむし (kemushi)

けいと (keito)

けんだま (kendama)

けいかん (keikan)

け (ke)

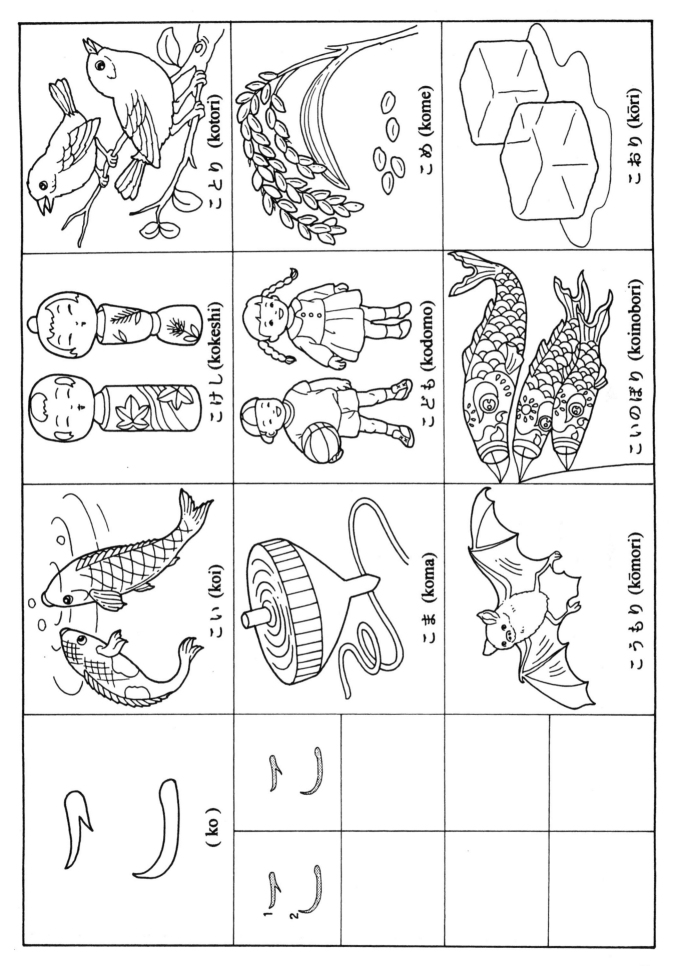

ことり (kotori)

こめ (kome)

こおり (kōri)

こけし (kokeshi)

こども (kodomo)

こいのぼり (koinobori)

こい (koi)

こま (koma)

こうもり (kōmori)

(ko)

11

さめ (same)	さくらんぼ (sakuranbo)	さいころ (saikoro)
さら (sara)	さかな (sakana)	さんかく (sankaku)
さくら (sakura)	さむらい (samurai)	さいふ (saifu)
さ (sa)	サ	

しか (shika)	しおり (shiori)	しかく (shikaku)
しんかんせん (shinkansen)	しんぶん (shinbun)	しっぽ (shippo)
しろ (shiro)	しまうま (shimauma)	しんごう (shingō)

し (shi)

し　し

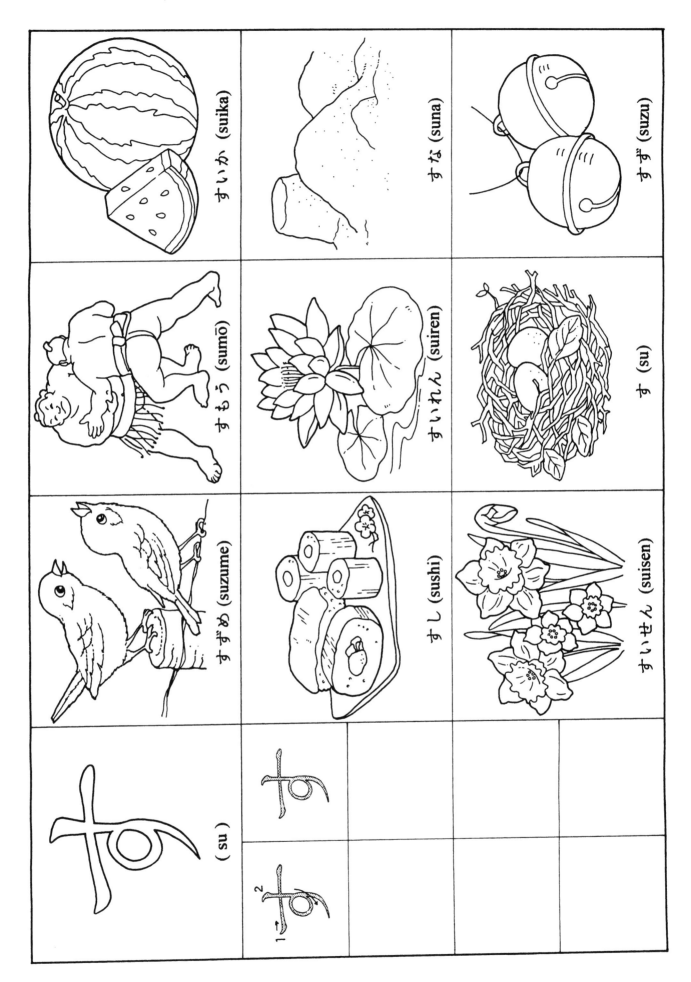

すいか (suika)

すな (suna)

すず (suzu)

すもう (sumō)

すいれん (suiren)

す (su)

すずめ (suzume)

すし (sushi)

すいせん (suisen)

（su）

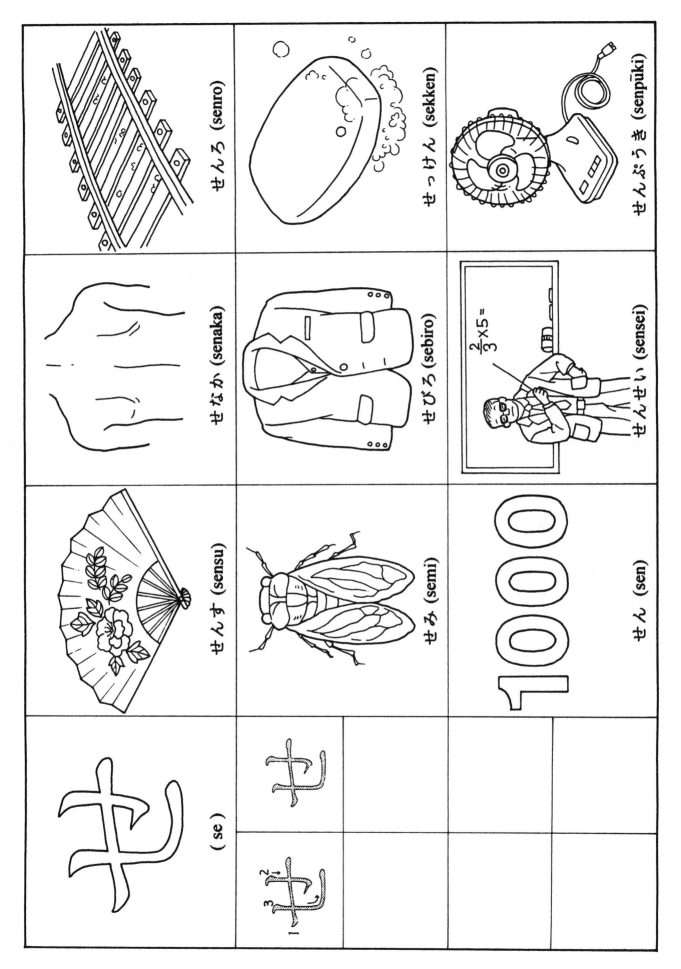

せんろ (senro)

せっけん (sekken)

せんぷうき (senpūki)

せなか (senaka)

せびろ (sebiro)

せんせい (sensei)

$\frac{2}{3} \times 5 =$

せんす (sensu)

せみ (semi)

せん (sen)

1000

(se)

そり (sori)	ぞう (zō)	ぞうり (zōri)
そば (soba)	そうじき (sōjiki)	そろばん (soroban)
そら (sora)	そらまめ (soramame)	そで (sode)

そ (so)

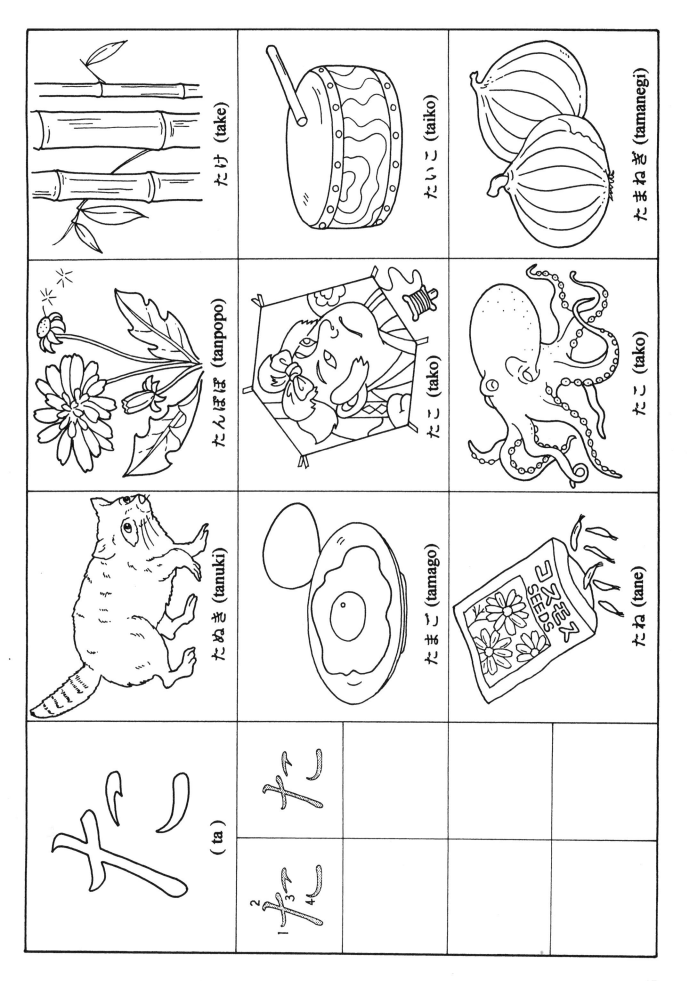

たけ (take)

たいこ (taiko)

たまねぎ (tamanegi)

たんぽぽ (tanpopo)

たこ (tako)

たこ (tako)

たぬき (tanuki)

たまご (tamago)

たね (tane)

コスモス
SEEDS

(ta)

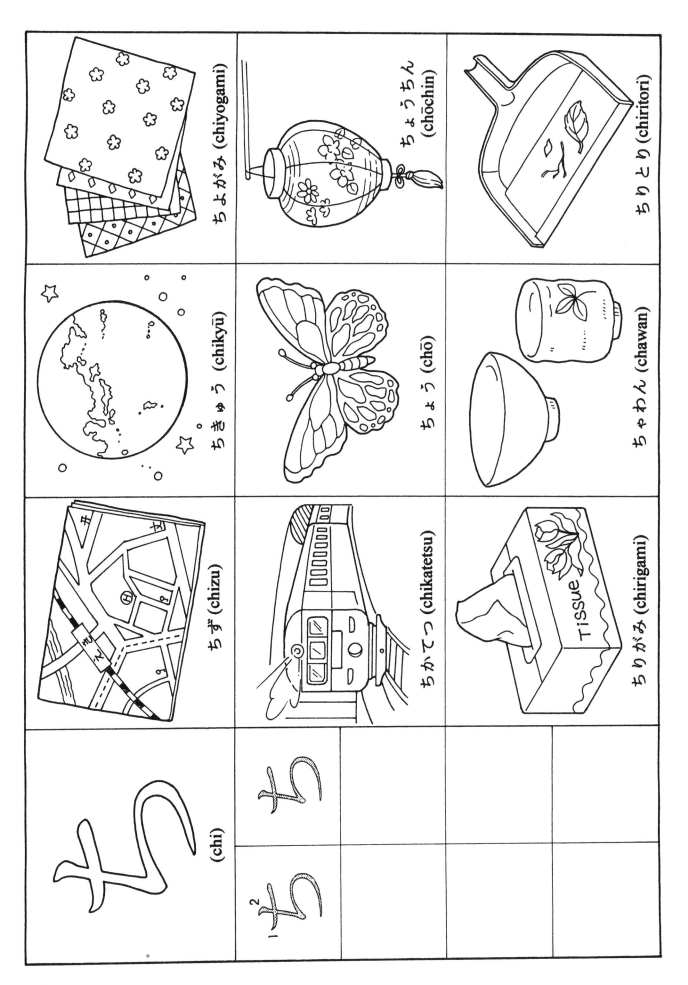

ちよがみ (chiyogami)

ちょうちん (chōchin)

ちりとり (chiritori)

ちきゅう (chikyū)

ちょう (chō)

ちゃわん (chawan)

ちず (chizu)

ちかてつ (chikatetsu)

ちりがみ (chirigami)

(chi)

つくえ (tsukue)

つめ (tsume)

つけもの (tsukemono)

つみき (tsumiki)

つばめ (tsubame)

つの (tsuno)

つる (tsuru)

つぼ (tsubo)

つき (tsuki)

(tsu)

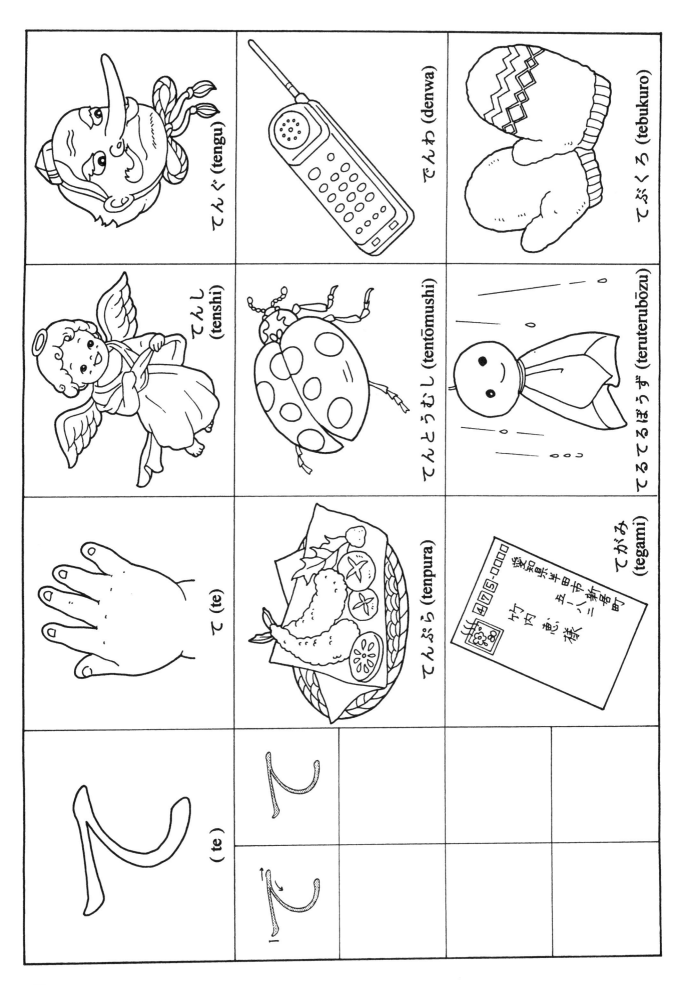

てんぐ (tengu)

でんわ (denwa)

てぶくろ (tebukuro)

てんし (tenshi)

てんとうむし (tentōmushi)

てるてるぼうず (teruterubōzu)

て (te)

てんぷら (tenpura)

てがみ (tegami)

(te)

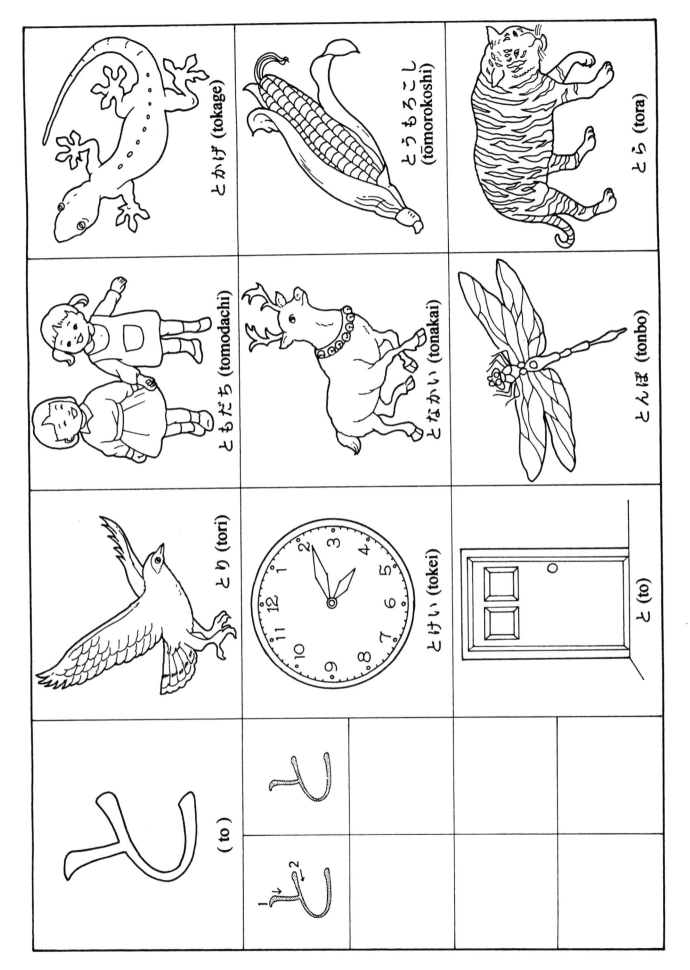

とかげ (tokage)

とうもろこし (tōmorokoshi)

とら (tora)

ともだち (tomodachi)

となかい (tonakai)

とんぼ (tonbo)

とり (tori)

とけい (tokei)

と (to)

と (to)

なべ (nabe)

なみ (nami)

なまえ (namae)

ながぐつ (nagagutsu)

なし (nashi)

なわ (nawa)

なす (nasu)

なわとび (nawatobi)

なみだ (namida)

な (na)

22

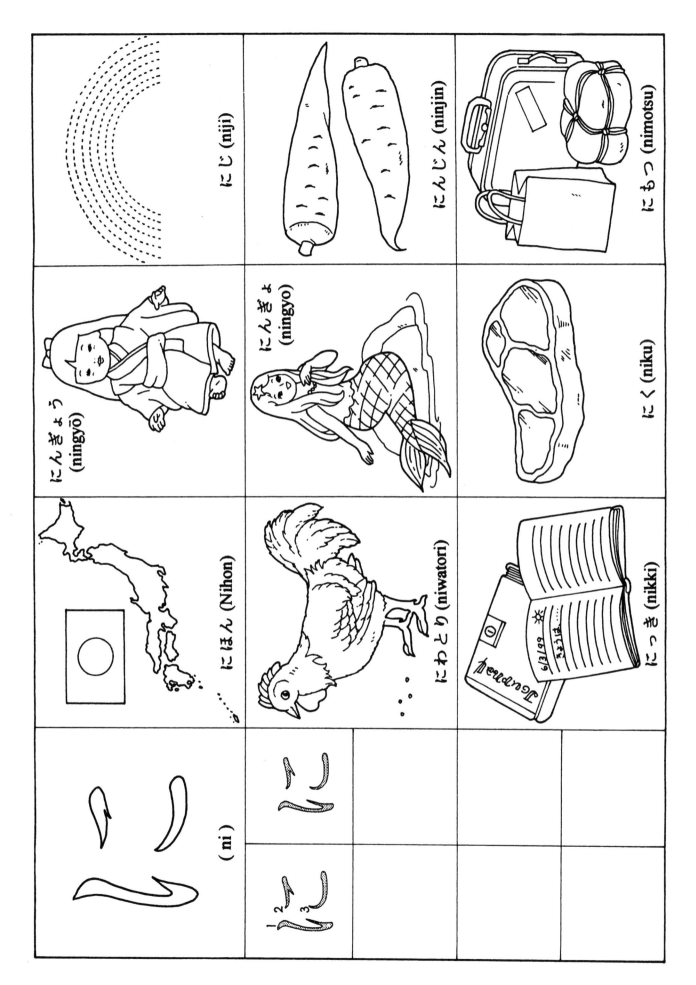

にじ (niji)

にんじん (ninjin)

にもつ (nimotsu)

にんぎょう (ningyō)

にんぎょ (ningyo)

にく (niku)

にほん (Nihon)

にわとり (niwatori)

にっき (nikki)

(ni)

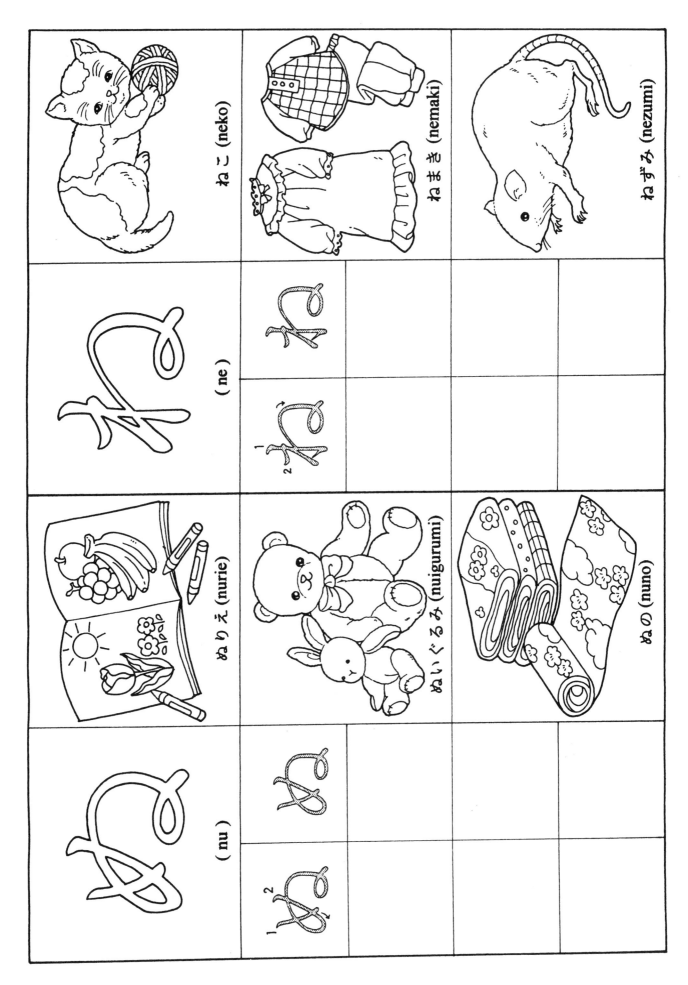

ねこ (neko)

ねまき (nemaki)

ねずみ (nezumi)

(ne)

ぬりえ (nurie)

ぬいぐるみ (nuigurumi)

ぬの (nuno)

(nu)

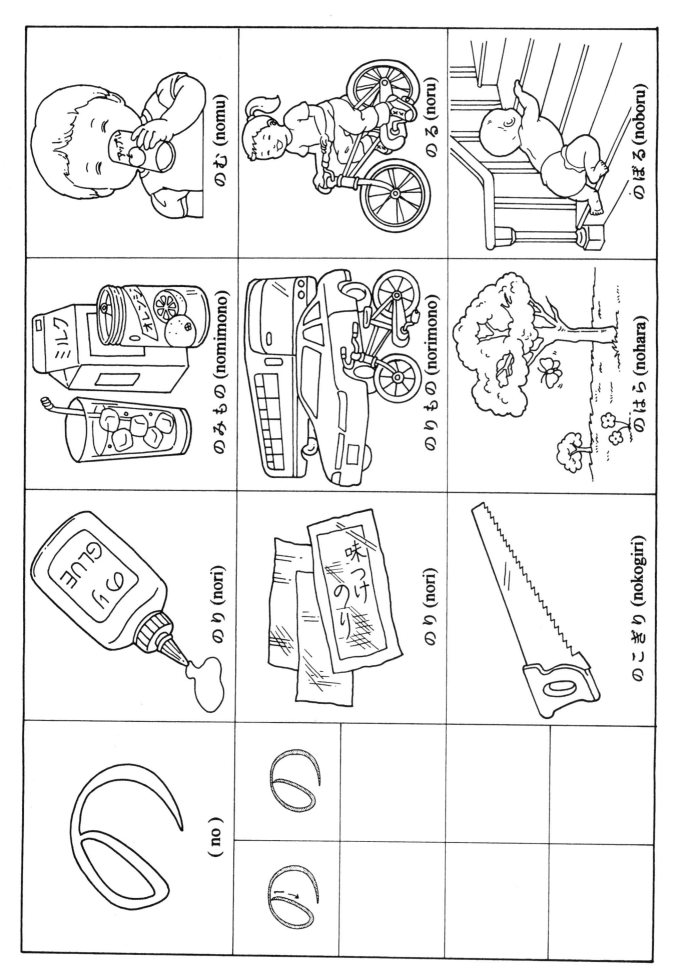

のむ (nomu)

のる (noru)

のぼる (noboru)

のみもの (nomimono)

のりもの (norimono)

のはら (nohara)

のり (nori)

のり (nori)

のこぎり (nokogiri)

(no)

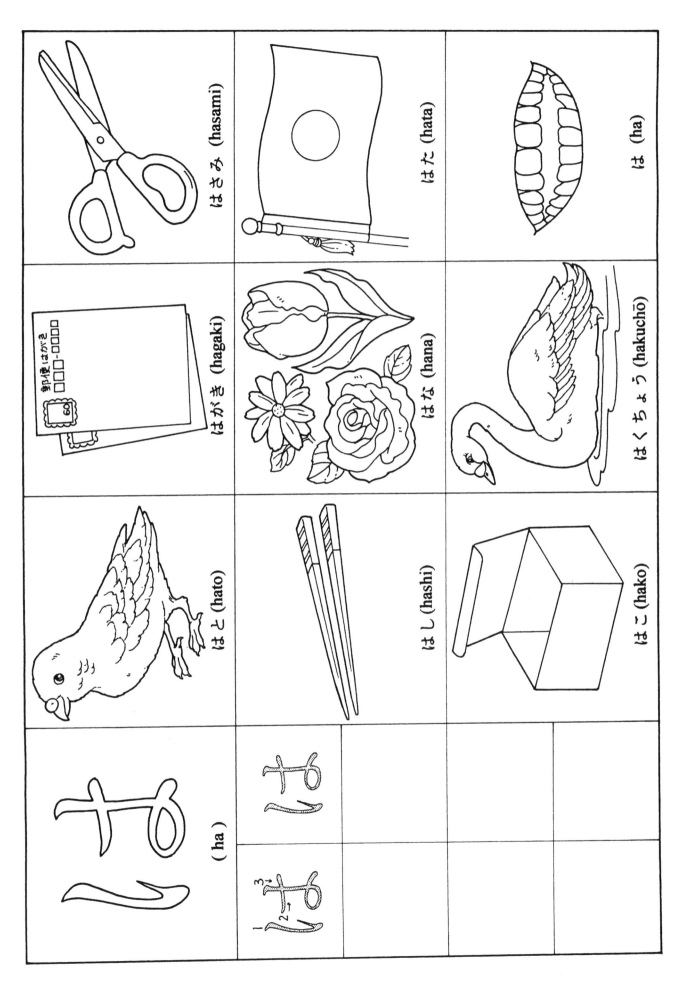

はさみ (hasami)

はた (hata)

は (ha)

はがき (hagaki)

はな (hana)

はくちょう (hakuchō)

はと (hato)

はし (hashi)

はこ (hako)

(ha)

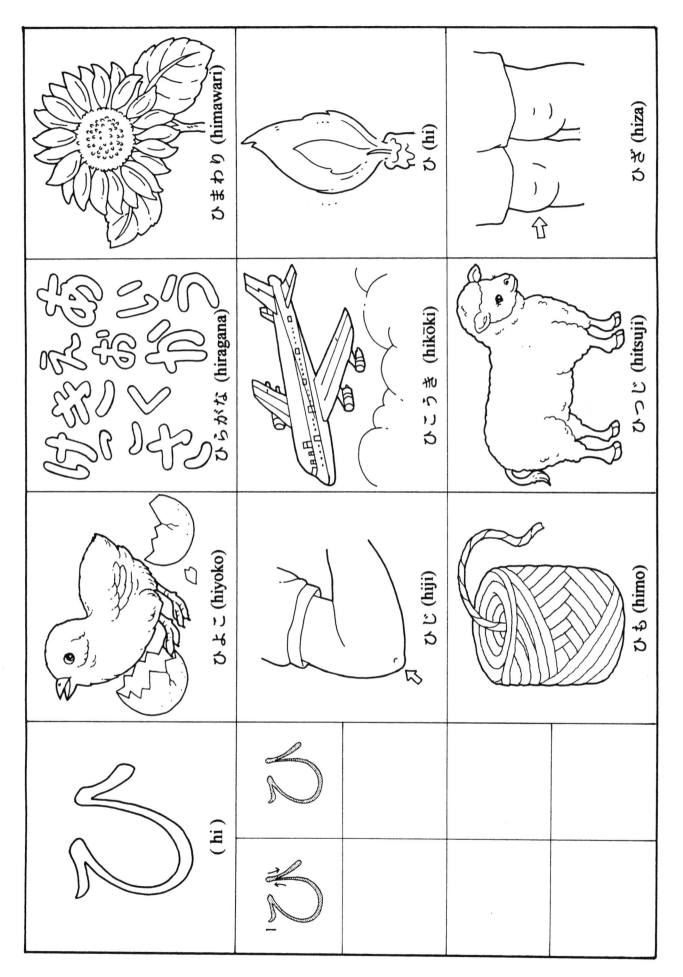

ひまわり (himawari)

ひ (hi)

ひざ (hiza)

ひらがな (hiragana)

ひこうき (hikōki)

ひつじ (hitsuji)

ひよこ (hiyoko)

ひじ (hiji)

ひも (himo)

ひ (hi)

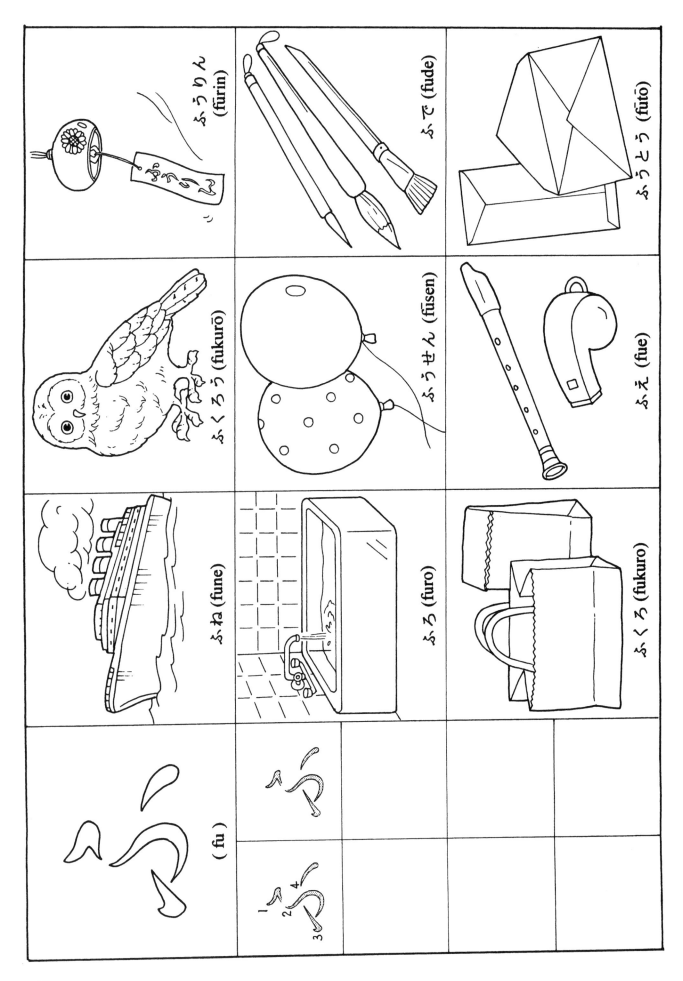

ふうりん (fūrin)

ふで (fude)

ふうとう (fūtō)

ふくろう (fukurō)

ふうせん (fūsen)

ふえ (fue)

ふね (fune)

ふろ (furo)

ふくろ (fukuro)

(fu)

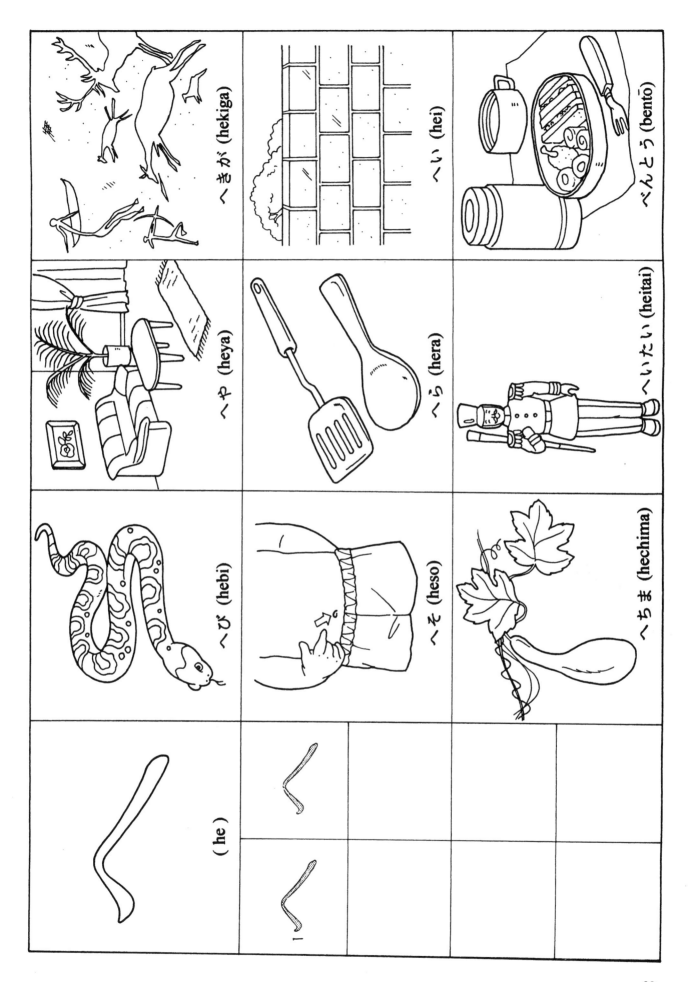

へきが (hekiga)

へい (hei)

べんとう (bentō)

へや (heya)

へら (hera)

へいたい (heitai)

へび (hebi)

へそ (heso)

へちま (hechima)

(he)

29

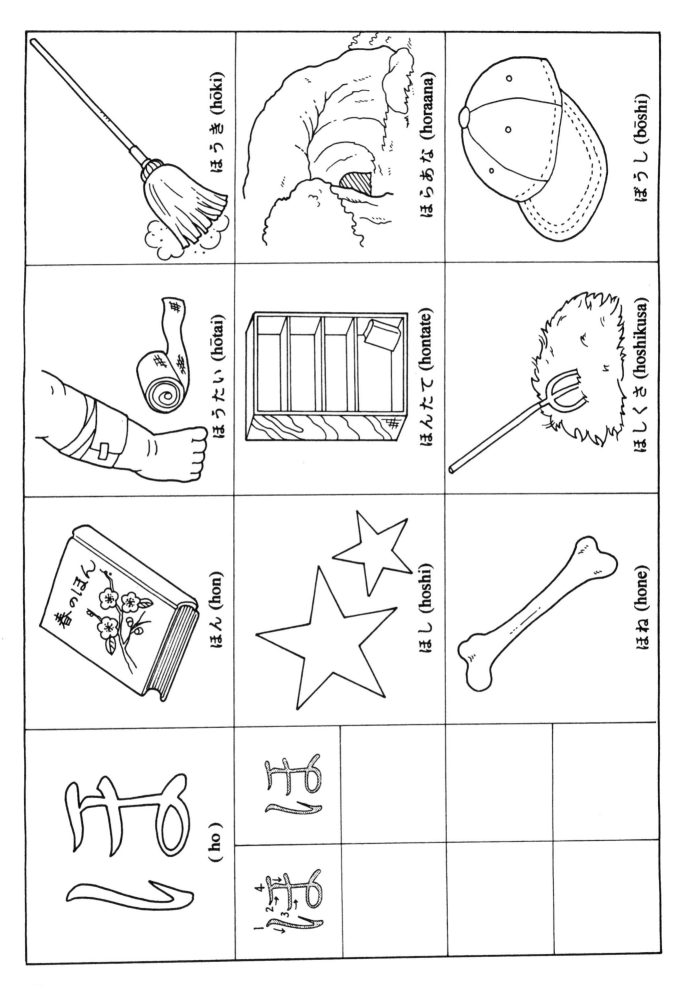

ほうき (hōki)

ほらあな (horaana)

ぼうし (bōshi)

ほうたい (hōtai)

ほんたて (hontate)

ほしくさ (hoshikusa)

ほん (hon)

ほし (hoshi)

ほね (hone)

ほ (ho)

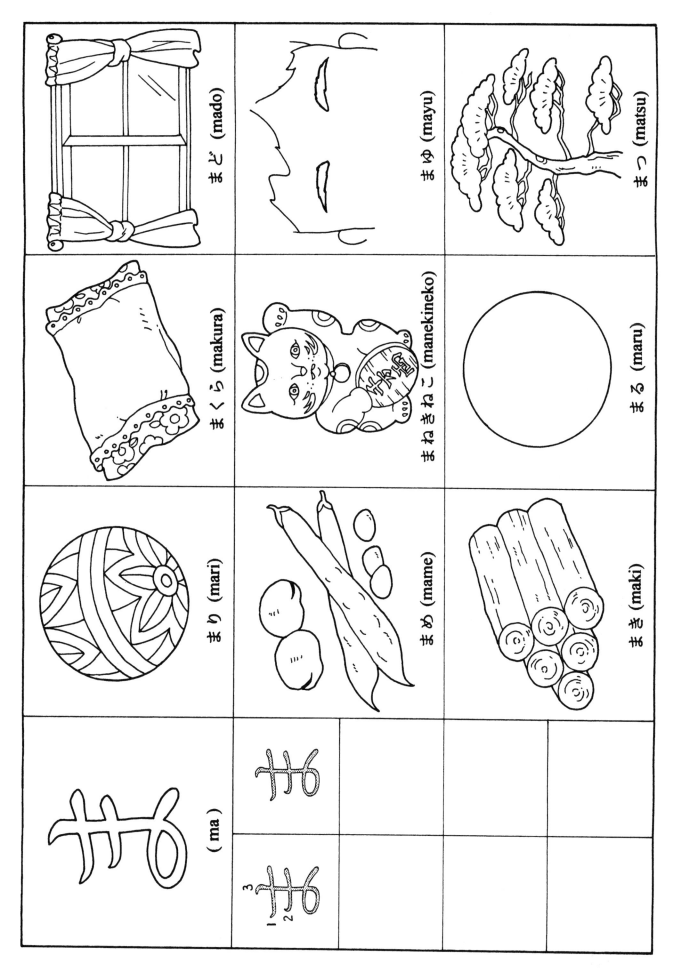

まど (mado)

まゆ (mayu)

まつ (matsu)

まくら (makura)

まねきねこ (manekineko)

まる (maru)

まり (mari)

まめ (mame)

まき (maki)

ま (ma)

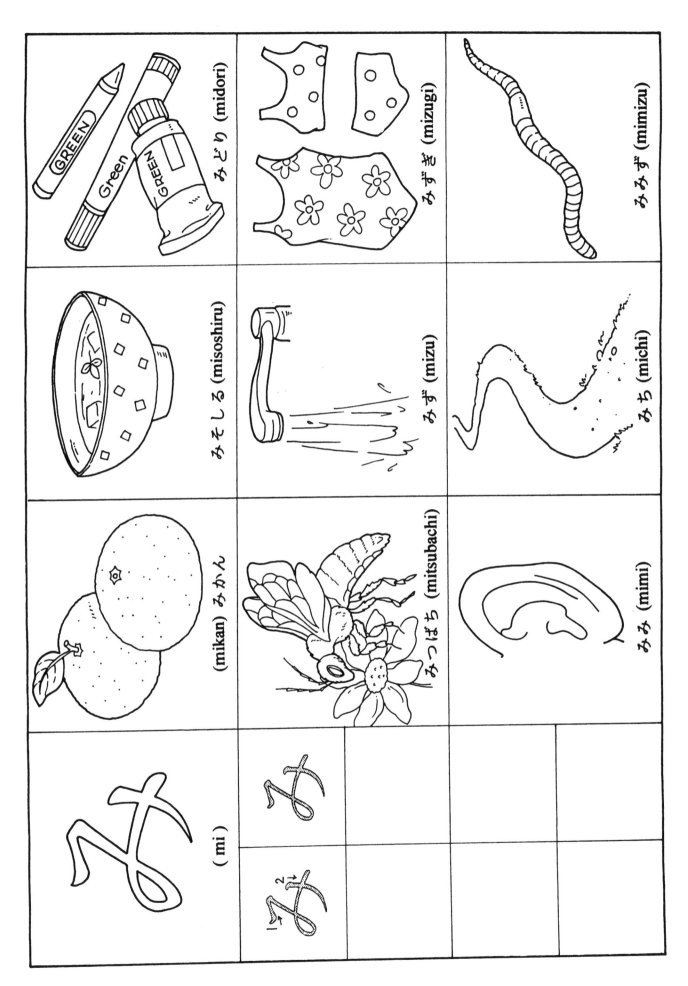

みどり (midori)

みずぎ (mizugi)

みみず (mimizu)

みそしる (misoshiru)

みず (mizu)

みち (michi)

みかん (mikan)

みつばち (mitsubachi)

みみ (mimi)

（ mi ）

め (me)	め (me)	めがね (megane)
(me)		
むし (mushi)	むしめがね (mushimegane)	むぎわらぼうし (mugiwarabōshi)
(mu)		

33

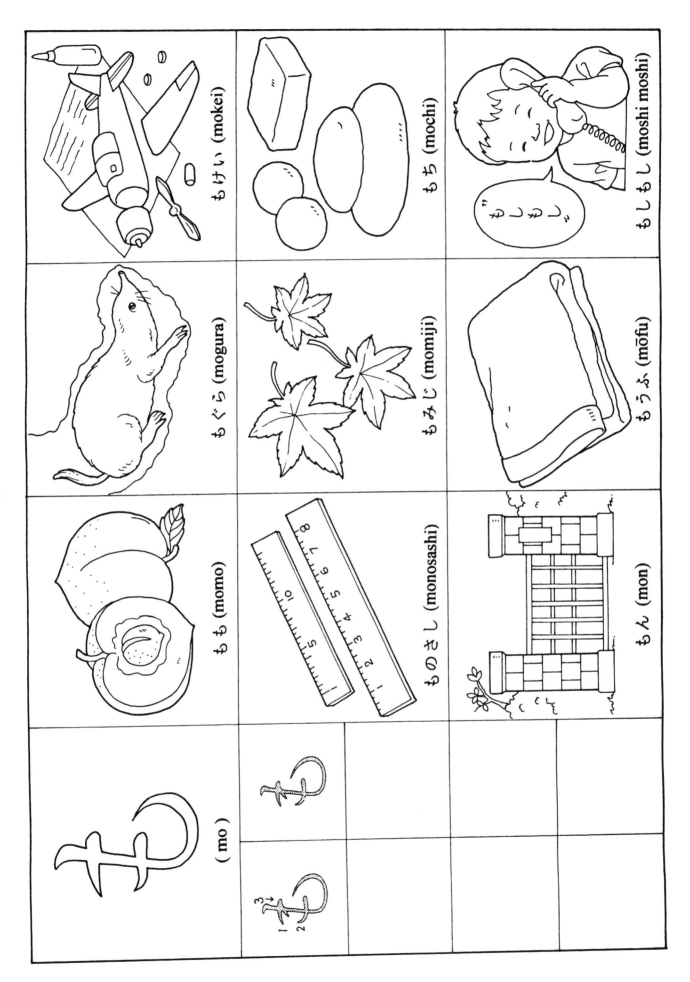

もけい (mokei)

もち (mochi)

もしもし (moshi moshi)

もぐら (mogura)

もみじ (momiji)

もうふ (mōfu)

もも (momo)

ものさし (monosashi)

もん (mon)

（mo）

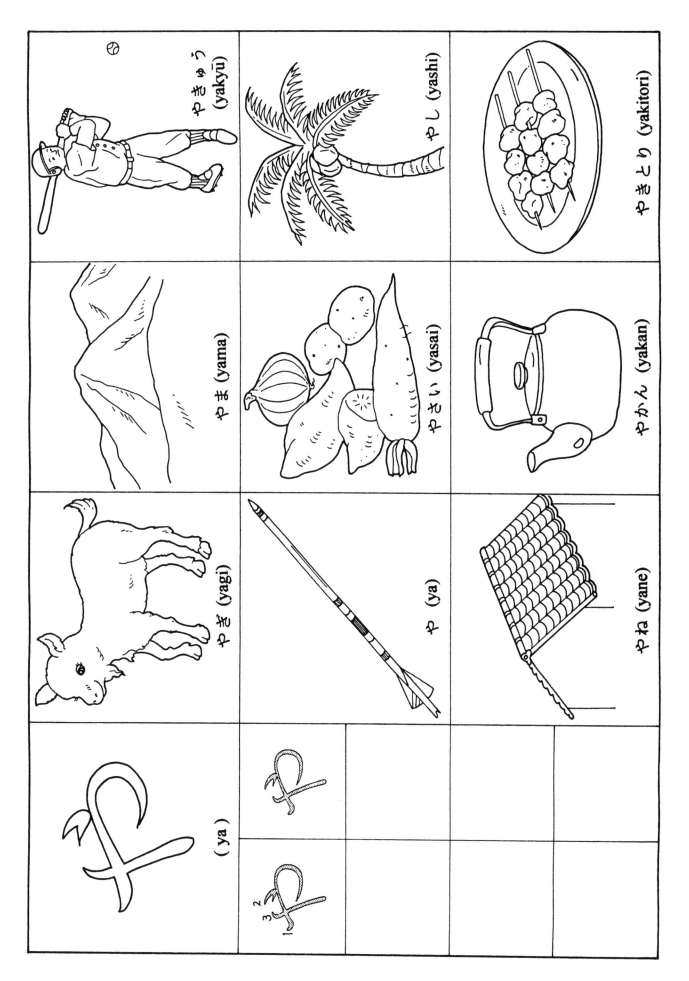

やきゅう (yakyū)

やし (yashi)

やきとり (yakitori)

やま (yama)

やさい (yasai)

やかん (yakan)

やぎ (yagi)

や (ya)

やね (yane)

(ya)

ゆび (yubi)

ゆびわ (yubiwa)

ゆかた (yukata)

ゆのみ (yunomi)

ゆり (yuri)

ゆりかご (yurikago)

ゆ (yu)

ゆき (yuki)

ゆきだるま (yukidaruma)

(yu)

らくだ (rakuda)

らっぱ (rappa)

らん (ran)

ら (ra)

よる (yoru)

ようせい (yōsei)

ようふく (yōfuku)

よ (yo)

さる (saru)	かえる (kaeru)	くるま (kuruma)
（ru）	る	る
りんご (ringo)	りす (risu)	りゅう (ryū)
（ri）	り	り

38

ろば (roba)	ろうそく (rōsoku)	ろっかくけい (rokkakukei)
ろ (ro)	ろ ろ	
れい (rei)	れっしゃ (ressha)	れいぞうこ (reizōko)
れ (re)	れ れ	

うたを うたう (uta o utau)	を (o)	わし (washi)	わ (wa)
ほんを よむ (hon o yomu)		わなげ (wanage)	
えを かく (e o kaku)		わに (wani)	

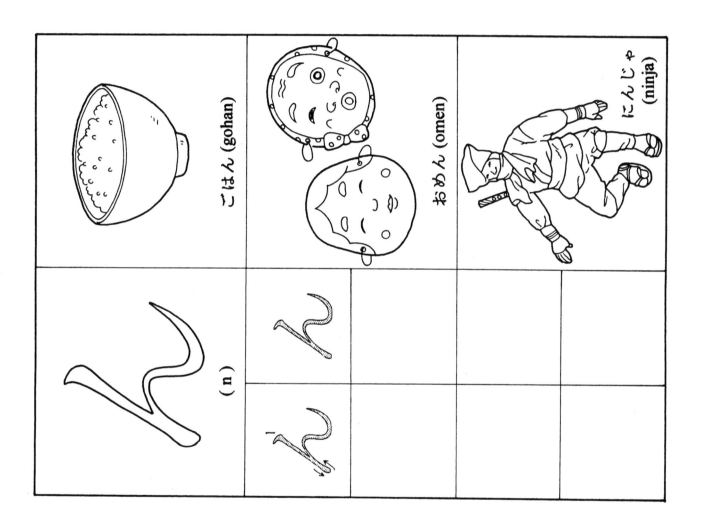

ごはん (gohan)

おめん (omen)

にんじゃ (ninja)

（ん）

Japanese/English Word List

p. 11

こ (ko)
こい	(koi) carp
こま	(koma) top
こうもり	(kōmori) bat
こけし	(kokeshi) *kokeshi* doll
こども	(kodomo) child, children
こいのぼり	(koinobori) carp-flag
ことり	(kotori) small bird
こめ	(kome) rice
こおり	(kōri) ice

p. 12

さ (sa)
さくら	(sakura) cherry blossoms
さむらい	(samurai) Japanese swordsman
さいふ	(saifu) wallet
さら	(sara) dish, plate
さかな	(sakana) fish
さんかく	(sankaku) triangle
さめ	(same) shark
さくらんぼ	(sakuranbo) cherry
さいころ	(saikoro) die, dice

p. 13

し (shi)
しろ	(shiro) castle
しまうま	(shimauma) zebra
しんごう	(shingō) traffic light
しんかんせん	(shinkansen) (Japanese) bullet train
しんぶん	(shinbun) newspaper
しっぽ	(shippo) tail
しか	(shika) deer
しおり	(shiori) bookmark
しかく	(shikaku) square

p. 14

す (su)
すずめ	(suzume) sparrow
すし	(sushi) *sushi*
すいせん	(suisen) daffodil, narcissus
すもう	(sumō) *sumo* wrestling
すいれん	(suiren) water lily
す	(su) nest
すいか	(suika) watermelon
すな	(suna) sand
すず	(suzu) bell

p. 15

せ (se)
せんす	(sensu) (folding) fan
せみ	(semi) cicada
せん	(sen) a thousand
せなか	(senaka) back
せびろ	(sebiro) business suit
せんせい	(sensei) teacher
せんろ	(senro) (railroad) line, track
せっけん	(sekken) soap
せんぷうき	(senpūki) electric fan

p. 16

そ (so)
そら	(sora) sky
そらまめ	(soramame) bean
そで	(sode) sleeve
そば	(soba) buckwheat noodles
そうじき	(sōjiki) vacuum cleaner
そろばん	(soroban) abacus
そり	(sori) sled

ぞ (zo)
| ぞう | (zō) elephant |
| ぞうり | (zōri) Japanese sandals |

p. 17

た (ta)
たぬき	(tanuki) raccoon dog
たまご	(tamago) egg
たね	(tane) seed
たんぽぽ	(tanpopo) dandelion
たこ	(tako) kite
たこ	(tako) octopus
たけ	(take) bamboo
たいこ	(taiko) drum
たまねぎ	(tamanegi) onion

p. 18

ち (chi)
ちず	(chizu) map
ちかてつ	(chikatetsu) subway
ちりがみ	(chirigami) tissue
ちきゅう	(chikyū) earth
ちょう	(chō) butterfly
ちゃわん	(chawan) (rice) bowl, teacup
ちよがみ	(chiyogami) *origami* paper with pattern
ちょうちん	(chōchin) (paper) lantern
ちりとり	(chiritori) dustpan

p. 19

つ (tsu)
つる	(tsuru) crane
つぼ	(tsubo) jar, pot
つき	(tsuki) moon
つみき	(tsumiki) (building) blocks
つばめ	(tsubame) swallow
つの	(tsuno) horn
つくえ	(tsukue) desk
つめ	(tsume) (finger) or (toe) nail
つけもの	(tsukemono) pickles

p. 20

て (te)
て	(te) hand
てんぷら	(tenpura) deep-fried food
てがみ	(tegami) letter
てんし	(tenshi) angel
てんとうむし	(tentōmushi) ladybug
てるてるぼうず	(teruterubōzu) paper doll to bring fine weather

てんぐ	(tengu) long-nosed goblin	のみもの	(nomimono) drink
でんわ	(denwa) telephone	のりもの	(norimono) vehicle
てぶくろ	(tebukuro) mittens, gloves	のはら	(nohara) field

p. 21

と (to)
とり	(tori) bird	のむ	(nomu) to drink
とけい	(tokei) clock, watch	のる	(noru) to ride
と	(to) door	のぼる	(noboru) to climb
ともだち	(tomodachi) friend		
となかい	(tonakai) reindeer		
とんぼ	(tonbo) dragonfly		
とかげ	(tokage) lizard		
とうもろこし	(tōmorokoshi) corn		
とら	(tora) tiger		

p. 26

は (ha)
はと	(hato) pigeon, dove
はし	(hashi) chopsticks
はこ	(hako) box
はがき	(hagaki) postal card
はな	(hana) flower
はくちょう	(hakuchō) swan
はさみ	(hasami) scissors
はた	(hata) flag
は	(ha) tooth

p. 22

な (na)
なす	(nasu) eggplant
なわとび	(nawatobi) jump rope
なみだ	(namida) tears
ながぐつ	(nagagutsu) boots
なし	(nashi) pear
なわ	(nawa) rope
なべ	(nabe) pot
なみ	(nami) wave
なまえ	(namae) name

p. 27

ひ (hi)
ひよこ	(hiyoko) chick
ひじ	(hiji) elbow
ひも	(himo) cord
ひらがな	(hiragana) *hiragana*
ひこうき	(hikōki) airplane
ひつじ	(hitsuji) sheep
ひまわり	(himawari) sunflower
ひ	(hi) fire
ひざ	(hiza) knee

p. 23

に (ni)
にほん	(Nihon) Japan
にわとり	(niwatori) hen, chicken
にっき	(nikki) diary
にんぎょう	(ningyō) doll
にんぎょ	(ningyo) mermaid
にく	(niku) meat
にじ	(niji) rainbow
にんじん	(ninjin) carrot
にもつ	(nimotsu) luggage

p. 28

ふ (fu)
ふね	(fune) ship
ふろ	(furo) bath
ふくろ	(fukuro) bag
ふくろう	(fukurō) owl
ふうせん	(fūsen) balloon
ふえ	(fue) flute, whistle
ふうりん	(fūrin) wind-bell
ふで	(fude) (paint)brush
ふうとう	(fūtō) envelope

p. 24

ぬ (nu)
ぬりえ	(nurie) coloring book
ぬいぐるみ	(nuigurumi) stuffed animal
ぬの	(nuno) cloth

ね (ne)
ねこ	(neko) cat
ねまき	(nemaki) nightwear
ねずみ	(nezumi) mouse

p. 29

へ (he)
へび	(hebi) snake
へそ	(heso) navel
へちま	(hechima) sponge gourd
へや	(heya) room
へら	(hera) spatula
へいたい	(heitai) soldier
へきが	(hekiga) wall painting
へい	(hei) stone wall
べんとう	(bentō) box lunch

p. 25

の (no)
のり	(nori) paste, glue
のり	(nori) papery seaweed
のこぎり	(nokogiri) saw

ろ (ro)	ろば	(roba) donkey	を (o)	うたを うたう	(uta o otau) to sing a song
	ろうそく	(rōsoku) candle		ほんを よむ	(hon o yomu) to read a book
	ろっかくけい	(rokkakukei) hexagon		えを かく	(e o kaku) to draw a picture

p. 40

わ (wa)	わし	(washi) eagle			
	わなげ	(wanage) quoits			
	わに	(wani) crocodile, alligator			

p. 41

ん (n)	ごはん	(gohan) cooked rice
	おめん	(omen) mask
	にんじゃ	(ninja) (Japanese) assassin

Index of English Words